Peter Paul

Rubens

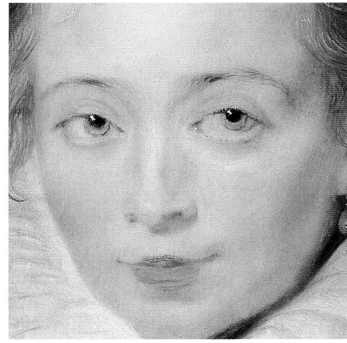

Layout: Julien Depaulis
Cover: Stéphanie Angoh

ISBN 1 90431 085 0

© Confidential Concepts, worldwide, USA, 2003
© Sirrocco, London, 2003 (English version)

Printed in Hong Kong

Peter Paul

Rubens

Sirrocco

The name of the great seventeenth-century Flemish painter Peter Paul Rubens is known throughout the world. The importance of his contribution to the development of European culture is generally recognized. The perception of life that he revealed in his pictures is so vivid, and fundamental human values are affirmed in them with such force, that we look on Rubens' paintings as a living aesthetic reality of our own time as well.

One gains the impression that in the seventeenth century Rubens did not attract as much attention as later. This may appear strange: indeed his contemporaries praised him as the "Apelles of our day". However, in the immediate years after the artist's death in 1640 the reputation which he had gained throughout Europe was overshadowed. The reasons for this can be found in the changing historical situation in Europe during the latter half of the seventeenth century. In the first decades of that century nations and absolutist states were rapidly forming. Rubens' new approach to art could not fail to serve as a mirror for the most diverse social strata in many European countries which were keen to assert their national identity and had followed the same path of development. This aim was inspired by Rubens' idea that the sensually perceived material world had value in itself; Rubens' lofty conception of man, his place in the Universe, and his emphasis on the sublime tension of man's physical and imaginative powers (born in conditions of the most bitter social conflicts), became a kind of banner of this struggle, and provided an ideal worth fighting for. In the second half of the seventeenth century the political situation in Europe was different. In Germany after the end of the Thirty Years' War, in France following the Frondes, and in England as the result of the Restoration, the absolutist regime triumphed. There was an increasing disparity in society between conservative and progressive forces; and this led to a "re-assessment of values" among the privileged, who were reactionary by inclination, and to the emergence of an ambiguous and contradictory attitude towards Rubens.

1. ***The Adoration of the Shepherds***. 1608,
    oil on canvas,
    63.5 x 47 cm,
    The Hermitage,
    St. Petersburg.

2. ***Self-Portrait***.
    Kunsthistorisches
    Museum, Vienna.

This attitude became as internationally prevalent as his high reputation during his lifetime, and this is why we lose trace of many of the artist's works in the second half of the seventeenth century after they left the hands of their original owners (and why there is only rare mention of his paintings in descriptions of the collections of this period). Only in the eighteenth century did Rubens' works again attract attention.

In the course of the three centuries which have elapsed since the death of Rubens, his artistic legacy, while not losing its immediate aesthetic value, has been variously interpreted. Prevailing aesthetic opinion has never been able to ignore his influence, but at each specific historical juncture it has sought to channel this influence in a particular direction. At times the perception and interpretation of the artist's legacy has been determined by those features which people desired to see in his works, or those that they hesitated to find there. Rubens' creative activities were so closely interwoven with the world he lived in that the detachment necessary for an overall assessment of his role and importance was not possible to achieve during his lifetime.
His contemporaries did not furnish literature on his art.
Only a few brief reviews or verses dedicated to his works by his contemporaries confirm his wide recognition.[1]

The opinion stated in a letter by Vincenzo Giustiniani, the well-known Italian *Maecenas* and patron of Caravaggio, may be considered one of the first attempts to define the nature of the artist's work. Writing during Rubens' lifetime, Giustiniani discussed the development of contemporary art: he considered it possible to place Caravaggio and Guido Reni in one group, with Rubens in another. He included Rubens, together with Ribera, Terbrugghen and Honthorst, in the group of "naturalists".[2]

Critical writings about Rubens began to appear when enthusiasm for him was moderated, and when the aesthetics of the "Grand Manner" began to take hold.

One of the chief proponents of this trend was Giovanni Pietro Bellori, the director of the Academy of St. Luke in Rome. His classical theories had a decisive influence on the formation of artistic taste throughout Europe in the second half of the eighteenth century. According to his aesthetic principles, the main requirement of art was that it should embody "the ideal of beauty"; moreover, all that was individual, partial, accidental or transitory had to be raised to the level of the universal, eternal and immutable.

3. *Head of an Old Man*. around 1609, oil on wood, 63.5 x 50.2 cm, The Hermitage, St. Petersburg.

4. ***The Coronation of the Virgin***. Around 1609-1611, oil on canvas, 106 x 78 cm, The Hermitage, St. Petersburg.

5. ***Virgin and Child in a Garland***. Alte Pinakothek, Munich.

6. ***Roman Charity.***
   Around 1612,
   oil on canvas,
   140.5 x 180.3 cm,
   The Hermitage,
   St. Petersburg.

7. ***Christ with the
   Crown of Thorns***
   (Ecce homo). Before
   1612, oil on wood,
   125.7 x 96.5 cm,
   The Hermitage,
   St. Petersburg.

8. ***Jupiter and Callisto***.
1613, oil on wood,
126.5 x 187 cm,
Gemäldegalerie Alte
Meister, Cassel.

Rubens, with his concrete observation of his life and sensualistic approach, was seen as an underminer of such canons, and as an offender of social decorum (although, even so, he impressed Bellori in many ways).[3]

At the end of the seventeenth century Roger de Piles, a recognized art specialist and leader of the "Rubensistes" (a new tendency in French painting and the theory of art) praised Rubens as a brilliant master of colour. Like adherents of the hedonist aesthetics in the eighteenth century, Roger de Piles considered colour as the "spirit of painting" and "the satisfaction of the eyes" as the basic purpose of art.[4]

With the approach of the French Revolution of 1789, however, new movements of artistic theories grew, and Neo-Classicism was being formed. Its theoretician, Johann-Joachim Winckelmann,[5] promoted it to counteract the "defiled" culture of the aristocratic drawing room. The rationalist aesthetics of his ideal, "the noble simplicity and calm majesty of free Greece", naturally rejected Rubens as he was then understood. It was to be expected, furthermore, that the artist's supposed hedonism was quite unacceptable to the severe civic-mindedness of the revolutionary Jacobin Classicism of David. In eighteenth-century Germany the protagonists of the "Sturm und Drang" period had already advanced concepts directed against the ancien régime which were also contrary to Classicism. They had declared the free development of the personality to be the sole source of artistic creativity and had regarded Rubens with joy.[6] Goethe, to the end of his days, considered Rubens to possess great virtues.[7]

These ideas were opposed by the narrow nationalist tendency in German Romanticism. The latter regarded the spiritual world of the Middle Ages, and the Gothic style as an expression of abstracted religious feeling, to be their ideal. For Friedrich Schlegel, Rubens was merely "an extremely misguided talent, and a false artistic innovator".[8]

The French Romantics of the early nineteenth century took a characteristically different attitude towards Rubens. Delacroix produced a veritable apotheosis of Rubens in his Journal.[9] The artist Eugene Fromentin who was a follower of Delacroix and passionate admirer of Flemish painting, compared Rubens' works to heroic poetry and wrote enthusiastically about the "radiant light of his ideas".[10]
In nineteenth-century Belgium, which had just won its independence, there was an ambiguous attitude to Rubens. The progressive democratic movement bore his name on its banner.

9. ***The Descent from the Cross***. Around 1612-1614, oil on wood, 48.7 x 52 cm, The Hermitage, St. Petersburg.

Andre van Hasselt, a poet and publicist, saw Rubens as the founder of the national school of painting; he revealed Rubens' importance in establishing a national self-awareness which had in turn shown the Flemish people the real possibility of their further advance.[11]

The view of official circles, however, was expressed by Van den Branden, the keeper of the Antwerp city archives. He complained that the artist had "endowed his figures with a heroic mobility and liveliness that was unsuitable for their setting in the peaceful temples of God". Van den Branden reproved Rubens with having betrayed the national character: for him, only the masters of the fifteenth century and Quentin Massys were the true exponents.[12]

The artist's Belgian biographer, Max Rooses, devoted his entire life to the collection of material relating to Rubens. He completed the major work of publishing Rubens' correspondence which he had begun with Charles Ruellens; it amounted to six volumes and included letters to and from Rubens, and those which discussed him.[13] To this day the publication has remained unique of its kind; only a very few letters by Rubens have been discovered since Rooses completed his work. The only exhaustive publication of Rubens' works is even now the fundamental catalogue compiled by Rooses, which includes all the then known paintings and drawings of the master.[14]

In gathering together Rubens' legacy, Rooses was continuing the work begun in 1830 by the English antiquarian, John Smith, who had produced a multi-volume catalogue devoted to the best known Dutch, Flemish and French artists.[15] The second volume of Smith's catalogue deals with Rubens and notes everything that the author, saw or heard concerning Rubens throughout his lifetime. Another book which is on a par with Smith's catalogue as the earliest record of its kind is C. G. Voorhelm-Schneevoogt's list of the engravings made from Rubens' paintings and published in 1873.[16]

By the end of the nineteenth century, art history as an independent field of research had begun to stand distinct from the broader study of culture as a whole. It was the publication in 1898 of Jakob Burckhardt's book

10. ***Venus and Adonis***.
Around 1614, oil on wood, 83 x 90.5 cm, The Hermitage, St. Petersburg.

Recollection of Rubens[17] that initiated the historico-cultural approach to the study of art. In his book the German scholar (who had worked in Switzerland) recognized and defined Rubens' aspiration towards the "extolling of man in all his capabilities and aspirations".

11. ***Three Graces Adorning Nature***.
1615, oil on canvas, 106.7 x 72.4 cm, Art Museum and Gallery, Glasgow.

12. ***Statue of Ceres***.
Around 1615, oil on wood, 90.5 x 65.5 cm, The Hermitage, St. Petersburg.

Burckhardt insisted that, in contrast to the theatricality and rhetoric of the Italians, Rubens' figures were true to life, and he laid emphasis not only on their formal qualities (of colour and chiaroscuro) but also on the importance of their moral and spiritual values.

Burckhardt presented extremely significant evidence of the close ties between Rubens and his native Antwerp, and showed that the substance of his portrayals had much in common with the outlook of those who were his most important and frequent patrons the influential city guilds and ecclesiastical fraternities. `

The scholar noted, with some pleasure, that "there was no royal throne in Rubens' immediate vicinity" and that "Antwerp was not a papal residence".

For Burckhardt, Rubens was the standard-bearer of the great new, universal flourishing of art which had been born in the Low Countries, the "Italy of the North", and continued the work begun during the Renaissance.

At the turn of the century there developed a more biased opinion that Rubens was a prophet of passive sensuality and nothing more.

However, both "art for art's sake" aesthetics and formal art criticism again acknowledged Rubens, since they saw in his art a degree of the primacy of form which they had proclaimed. In this respect interpretation of Rubens' artistic approach by the German scholar Rudolf Oldenbourg's was typical.[18] Although the formalist school was incapable of understanding the complex variety of artistic phenomena, it nevertheless played a great role in the history of art criticism. The actual study of Rubens' works, in particular, and of their specific "forms of expression" laid the foundations of contemporary Rubens studies.

By singling out the distinctive features of Rubens' artistic style it became possible to distinguish the master's own works from the enormous number of those produced under his direction, to establish who had influenced him, and to define the stages through which he had evolved. In short, it was possible to clarify the features of Rubens' individual creativity.

In the years between the two World Wars the work of Rubens was increasingly regarded as a direct expression of the anti-materialist and anti-realist trends that were identified with the feudal and absolutist Counter-Reformation in seventeenth-century Europe. The French historian Gabriel Hanotaux[19] emphasized the hedonistic sensuality and outward splendour of Rubens' art, considering that, by his very nature, this artist of elaborate spectacle was only suited to praise the monarchy and the church.

13. ***Bacchanalia***. Around 1615, oil on canvas, 91 x 107 cm, The Pushkin Museum of Fine Arts, Moscow.

Leo van Puyvelde, a Belgian art critic, imputed to Rubens a striving to transform the artistic image into a subjective world divorced from reality. "These creations are raised to such a high level", Puyvelde wrote in 1943, "that all the sounds of the real world have been muted."[20]

After the Second World War there was a notable return to an appreciation of the primary materials and actual circumstances of Rubens' art. Much has been achieved in this direction. First and foremost, the number of works known to be genuine Rubens has grown due to the inclusion of those that had been attributed to other painters or to unknown artists as well as quite unknown compositions, variants of already familiar pictures and preparatory works, drawings and sketches.

This has involved a reexamination of some previous conceptions of Rubens' development as an artist and adjustments to the datings. Entire periods and aspects of his artistic activities are now seen in a new light, and the gaps in the history of his artistic career are constantly decreasing.
To give examples: we have a quite different impression of Rubens as a draughtsman; his early pre-Italian works are more precisely placed; we understand better his relations with his predecessors and successors, and how his workshop was organized; and light has been shed on many iconographic problems, on the actual way in which he worked, and on the process whereby his conceptions were brought to life.

The following scholars have made major contributions to this development: G. Glück, W. R. Valentiner, L. Burchard, O. Benes, F. Lucht, J. S. Held, H. Gerson, M. Jaffé, R. A. d'Hulst, J. Millar, E. Haverkamp-Begemann, F. Baudouin, and O. Millar.

Rubens the man and his art are far more complex than were appreciated before. We now have an incomparably wider view of the artist's capabilities, and see a more varied range of sources from which he drew his inspiration and his different artistic tastes. While Rubens inherited the realist Flemish traditions of the art of Van Eyck and Brueghel, he was, at the same time, a loyal student of the Romanist master painters, the Antwerp Italianizers who had taken the achievements of the Italian Renaissance as their ideal. Following the example of his teachers, he travelled to Italy in 1600, when he was a young man of twenty-three, to be in direct communion with the treasures of ancient and Italian cultures. However, he approached what he had seen in Italy with a critical eye, and we may judge his true aspirations from what actually attracted him there.

14. *Two Satyrs*. Alte Pinakothek, Munich.

It was not so much Antique models of a formally strict and ideal beauty that drew Rubens: he preferred the relics of the late classical period and the sculpture of Hellenistic Rome, where "noble simplicity and calm majesty" were softened by the evocation of the living flesh Praxiteles' *Resting Satyr*, the *Laocoön, Heracles* of Farnese, and small decorative fountain work.

Rubens would return to the great art works and monuments he had seen in Italy more than once in his later artistic career. Among the Italian masters of the previous era he singled out the Venetians for their attachment to colour as the basic means of expression in painting, and Correggio with his sensuality and magical chiaroscuro. Rubens was enthralled by the dynamism of Leonardo da Vinci's *Battle near Anghiari*, and the titanic power of Michaelangelo's heroes. Rubens also took an interest in the expressiveness of the images in the work of Pordenone, an original but in no sense "great" master, attracted by his attempts to reconcile the ideal world of art with real life.

During Rubens' years in Italy Annibale Carracci, the head of the Academic school, was at the height of his reputation. Carracci's efforts to revive the objectivity of the Renaissance, its harmony of artistic vision, and to pay closer attention to the live model after the "excesses" of the mannerist approach, impressed Rubens. He was enraptured by Carracci's brilliant murals in Palazzo Farnese but in his own subsequent decorative works hardly followed this example. The small landscapes of Elsheimer (a German who had settled in Italy), on the other hand, which were pervaded by lyrical emotion, remained in Rubens' memory for a long time.

The innovative approach of the rebellious Caravaggio proved especially close to Rubens' heart. Caravaggio had demolished the abstracted character of religious painting by treating the conventional images and scenes from the ecclesiastical doctrine as earthly events, taking place among living people with real human concerns.

Consideration of his Italian contemporaries and a strong knowledge of the entire history of Italian art helped Rubens to find his own artistic idiom in which he addressed his Flemish compatriots on his return in 1609.

All the works that the produced here in the very first years (e.g. *The Adoration of the Magi* (p.79), Prado, Madrid; *The Elevation of the Cross* and *The Descent from the Cross* (p.32), Antwerp Cathedral), were executed with such a burning and passionate affirmation of life, permeated with such unsuppressed energy, and addressed the viewer with

15. ***Drunken Heracles***.
Oil on wood,
2.20 x 2m,
Gemäldegalerie,
Dresden.

such authority, that these canvases immediately outshone all the achievements of his Flemish predecessors.

Young artists began to flood towards Rubens' workshop from every corner of the country: he evidently had given expression to a feeling that had been maturing for a long time. His art flowed into the current of his compatriots' common interests and passions. It had organically become part of the affirmation and preservation of a common and distinct identity which Flanders had to create, finding itself once again part of the Spanish Empire of the Habsburgs after a stormy period of revolutionary struggle. Moreover, the political division of the Low Countries which resulted from the sixteenth-century revolution spurred a further need to give the separation from neighbouring Holland a spiritual and aesthetic expression.

In these circumstances the propaganda of the Catholic Counter-Reformation in Flanders took a distinctive form: while emphasizing their Catholicism as a countercharge to the Protestantism of the Dutch, the Flemish at the same time tried to secure their own place in the modern world and, in some degree, oppose the official outlook of the Vatican.

It should not be forgotten that the church commissions created in Rubens' workshop were not directed towards the Europe of the Counter-Reformation, but intended for Flemish churches.

One cannot speak of Rubens' "atheism", for he was a man of his time. Yet in his religious paintings there was no contradiction between the eternal divine values and those that were transitory and earthly. Rubens translated the abstracted dogmas of the church into the language of concrete living images; he likened the mystical meaning of Christ's sacrificial feat to entirely human virtues such as unyielding endurance and fearless selflessness (*The Descent from the Cross* (p.31-32); *The Crown of Thorns*).

The artist sought examples of elevated personal courage in ancient history, classical literature and mythology: it could be the public-spirited valour of the Romans Mucius Scaevola and Decius Mus; the self-sacrificing love of daughters (*Roman Charity*)(p.10); or the bold challenge to the monster which threatened to violate youth and beauty (*Perseus and Andromeda*)(p.45). Even traditional abstract allegories became brilliant embodiments of the vital and active forces of nature and the human spirit (*The Union of Earth and Water* (p.33); *Statue of Ceres*)(p.19). Having accepted the legacy of Italian art, Rubens remained a Flemish artist in the most specific qualities of his work. A wordly attention to detail and the palpably material quality of his images were the great legacy of his ancestors.

16. ***Hagar Leaves the House of Abraham***. 1615-1617, oil on wood, 62.8 x 72 cm, The Hermitage, St. Petersburg.

The inspired emotion of his works was the voice of contemporary Flemish or Netherlandish reality. Rubens demonstrated his predilection for native traditions in that he even departed from the techniques he had acquired in Italy after he returned to Flanders. He ceased to paint on canvas using dark underpainting and began to cultivate the old "Flemish style": he painted on wood, against light backgrounds, and in perfecting these methods achieved that resonant radiance of colour for which he is renowned.

Rubens' achievements as a master colourist and creator of images of a sensual beauty are acknowledged. Yet we must not forget that it is precisely to Rubens that we are beholden for a new, integral interpretation of the image of man.

Rubens refused to adopt the conventional and abstract mannerist conceptions of the human form and its movement; when he used such devices as contrapposto (the contrasting play of rest and motion) or depicted the *figura serpentinata* (snake-like posture), he tried not only to capture external movement, facial expression and bodily pose and gesture, but also to make it inaccordance with internal movement. Such a consistent psychological conditioning of the figure's movements was a direct elaboration of Renaissance accomplishments.

And it was Rubens' achievements that made possible the subsequent triumphs of Van Dyck's portrait painting and even the innovations of Rembrandt and Velázquez. After the creative flights of the first years following his return from Italy, Rubens had to tackle the task of organizing his workshop, arranging the principles of his artistic vision into a coherent system and reducing them to basic forms and types.

17. **Portrait of a Young Man**. 1616-1617, oil on wood, 60 x 49 cm, The Hermitage, St. Petersburg.

He undertook the writing of the alphabet of a new language, as it were; he began to bring together those elements from which he would build his universe. His resolution of this problem underlay his works executed during his so-called period of "Classicism", 1611-1615. Step by step he studied the animated dynamism of the human body, paying attention both to the movements of individual figures and to their interrelations.

18. ***Portrait of a Young Man***. Oil on wood, 56.2 x 47.3 cm, Gemäldegalerie Alte Meister, Cassel.

19. ***The Head of the Franciscan***. 1615-1617, oil on canvas, The Hermitage, St. Petersburg.

20. *Albert and Nicolas Rubens*.
Collection of the
Dukes of
Liechtenstein, Vaduz.

21. ***The Descent from
the Cross***. 1618,
oil on canvas,
297 x 200 cm,
The Hermitage,
St. Petersburg.

22. *The Descent from the Cross*. Antwerp Cathedral.

23. *The Union of Earth and Water*. Around 1618, oil on canvas, 222.5 x 180.5 cm, The Hermitage, St. Petersburg.

Persistently, stage by stage, he perfected his ability to convey the hidden drama and inner tension that guided any interplay between human figures. He wanted to communicate the unstable, volatile and mobile balancing of forces, or, to be more precise, the transient equilibrium of independent human volitions, which were then simply juxtaposed rather than opposed in conflict (*Roman Charity*)(p.10). It was only when he had resolved this task at the beginning of the 1620s that Rubens turned to the dynamic interaction of human crowds; he created powerful images executed with the sense of man's self-affirmation in his frenzied struggle against hostile forces.

It was then that his famous paintings of battles, of fights with wild animals or of bacchanalia appeared, spectacles of joyful celebration in the life forces inherent in human nature. Yet the human figure does not become lost or merged in these dynamic and turbulent compositions. In Rubens' works the human figure always retains an independent significance: it is always the mainspring of the action, the centre which attracts energy to itself, and the rallying-point in a general unity which is torn by contradictions.

The real content of the artist's paintings, whether religious or secular, was the purposeful human will that made its own way by solitary combat with the Universe.

It enlivens all around it, and subordinates all parts of the work to the expression of this basic idea. It is as if the force of the hero's passion, as he strives towards his goal, is embodied in the folds of his cloak which steams behind his shoulders (*Perseus and Andromeda*)(p.45). The strained efforts of the carters who, as they push their heavy cart with difficulty over the potholes of a mountain road, seem to encounter the resistance of the threatening cliffs that surround them and of the fantastically contorted trees, which like living beings, repel the invasion (*The Carters*)(p.38).Battles and hunts, scenes from classical mythology, Old Testament legends or stories from the life of Christ and the deeds of the saints, or representations of nature, all becomes the field of action in which man's creative will reveals itself.

The artist's portrait painting, in which he captured the characteristic features of a particular personality was also seen by him as the depiction of a protagonist in the same drama; he wanted to set down the individuality as expressed in an inimitable personal gesture which seemed to be an active and dynamic reaction to the impressions and influences (*Portrait of a Young Man*)(p.28-29).

24. ***Four Parts of the World***.
Kunsthistorisches Museum, Vienna.

However, the external plastic dynamism was but one of the stages in the development of Rubens' art. In the last ten years of his life Rubens moved from compositions which had been organized as a tangled mass of force and motion bursting into the pictorial expanse or striving to break its bounds (*Feast at the House of Simon the Pharisee*; *The Lion Hunt* (p.40); *Perseus and Andromeda*)(p.45) to those conceived as a different and new type of unity.

It was the unity of the energy of living beings that permeates the world, and the unity of the Universe itself of that extended material world in which this energy was in play. It is the very "corporeality" of the world in all its facets that now revealed itself before the artist, and took on a new expressiveness.

The themes of Rubens' works became calmer and more soothing. It was not the sense of the struggle for life which now resounded through the landscapes and mythological scenes but the fullness and beauty of life itself, which was worth struggling for and which was revealed to the viewer in all its brilliance. The image of man was only a part of the integral picture of the world created by the artist. Flowing movement was linked to the motion of colour and air which filled the universal expanse.
The precision of outline is blurred and the colours lose their local definition and isolation (*The Vision of St. Ildefonso*)(p.61-62). Compared to the cold brilliance and bright tonality of his early works, the colouring now became warmer and richer: the silvery-golden range is perceived almost as a single, blended coloured medium rich in nuance.

Yet human figures, as before, remained at the centre of the compositional and colouristic entity. The infinite space, air and light medium which surround them gave them a still greater significance (*Landscape with a Rainbow* (p.66); *Bacchus*)(p.74).
In this period of true artistic maturity Rubens fully appreciated his great predecessors Breughel and Titian, more than once drawing on their experience.
Rubens' artistic world, even in his easel works, seems either to burst beyond the frame or to entice the viewer into the depths of his vision. This to a great extent determines the expressiveness and power of his decorative works.

The illusory expanse of these decorative paintings is perceived as a continuation of the real world in which the viewer finds himself. That is how they achieve that enthralling emotional impact which makes the viewer sense that he is in direct contact with them. Furthermore, as a decorative artist Rubens never attempted a purely decorative approach.

25. ***Feast at the House of Simon the Pharisee***. 1620 (?), oil on canvas, 189 x 254.5 cm, The Hermitage, St. Petersburg.

26. ***The Carters***. Around
1620, oil on canvas,
86 x 126.5 cm,
The Hermitage,
St. Petersburg.

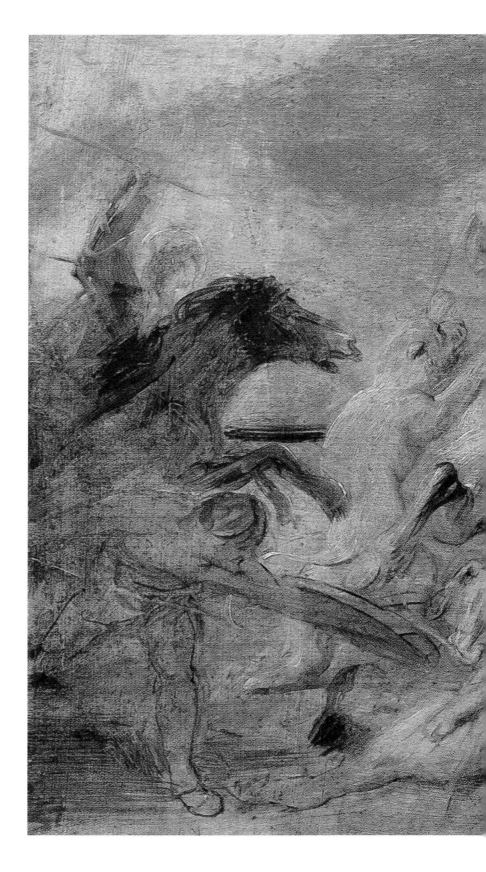

27. ***Lion Hunt***. Around
1621, oil on wood,
43 x 64 cm,
The Hermitage,
St. Petersburg.

28. ***The Garden of Love***.
    Prado, Madrid.

29. ***Portrait of Charles
    de Longueval***. 1621,
    oil on wood,
    62 x 50 cm,
    The Hermitage,
    St. Petersburg

In his series of paintings for official palatial residences in Paris and London, or in his decorative structures for the streets and squares of Antwerp to greet the Infante Ferdinand, the new Governor, Rubens wanted to say many things to the onlookers. Rubens knew how even the eulogistic conventions of a court order could be refreshed with a lively reference to contemporary events.

In his monumental paintings Rubens worked more on subjects of wide public concern. These were close to his own interests as an active public figure and as one who undertook important diplomatic assignments.

At times, he also resorted to the language of artistic imagery to bolster the language of diplomacy. When he was conducting negotiations in London in 1630 over the signing of a peace treaty between Spain and England, Rubens presented the English King with a painting on a topical theme, *Peace and War* (National Gallery, London). In 1638, powerless to halt the misfortunes which had befallen Europe, he painted *The Horrors of War* for the Duke of Tuscany (Uffizi, Florence), "that large-scale frontispiece to the Thirty Years' War," as Burckhardt called it.[21] In trying to express the current interests of his homeland when it was in difficult conditions, to a despotic foreign regime, Rubens was also inspired by the same tasks in his political activities as directed his hands as an artist: the patriotic tasks of national consolidation and self-affirmation.

The same purpose pervaded his activities as a connoisseur of ancient history, literature and classical artifacts. Rubens used the entire accumulation of eclectic pedantry that the late epigones of Renaissance humanism had accumulated to enrich his system of representation; in his hands it became a means whereby the discoveries of contemporary reality could find expression and urgent or even distressing ideas might be given artistic form.

In Rubens we do not see the follower of a tradition: he was a master who was able to apply the achievements of classical art to new tasks and in new conditions. Enriched by the understanding of the world in its sensual tangibility, infinity and mutability which had developed in the seventeenth century, Rubens used the experience of various contemporary artists to blaze his own trail to his personal goal.

Since he shared the life of his contemporaries and that of Europe as a whole, he was well aware of the leading idea of the period: not only the self-affirmation of the individual, but that of the nation as well.

30. *Perseus and Andromeda*. Early 1620s, oil on canvas, 99.5 x 139 cm, The Hermitage, St. Petersburg.

31. *Portrait of Marie de' Médici*. Louvre, Paris.

32. *Marie de' Médici
Represented as
Pallas*. 1622, oil
(grisalle) on wood,
22.5 x 15 cm.
The Hermitage,
St. Petersburg.

33. *The Coronation of Marie de' Médici*.
Louvre, Paris.

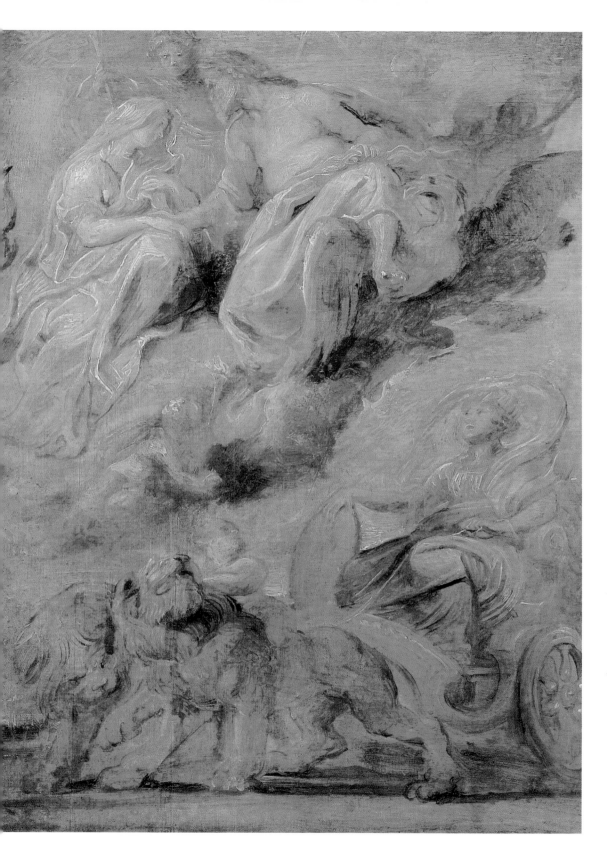

34. ***The Birth of Louis
    XIII***. Oil on canvas,
    394 x 295 cm,
    Louvre, Paris.

35. ***The Entry into
    Lyons***. 1622, oil on
    canvas (grisaille),
    33.5 x 24.2 cm,
    The Hermitage,
    St. Petersburg.

36. ***The Birth of the Dauphin***. 1622, oil on wood (grisaille), 33.6 x 24 cm, The Hermitage, St. Petersburg.

He also felt the drama of the inevitable struggle with those forces which opposed such self-affirmation. Nevertheless, his belief that the chosen goal was attainable allowed Rubens to perceive the final unity and harmony through an apparent chaos of discordant strivings. In Rubens' art we find all the aspects of seventeenth-century art: the frenzy of the Baroque, the harmony of Classicism, and the authenticity of Realism, subordinated to one idea: man's victorious triumph over the world.

37. ***The Coronation of the Queen***. 1622, oil on wood, 49 x 63 cm, The Hermitage, St. Petersburg.

BIOGRAPHY

1577

28 June: Born at Siegen in Westphalia (Germany); Peter Paul was the sixth child of Maria Pypelinckx and Jan Rubens, an Antwerp barrister who had fled from the Duke of Alba's reign of terror.

1578

The family moves to Cologne.

1589

After Jan Rubens' death his widow returns to Antwerp with their six children.

1589-1590

With his older brother Philip, Peter Paul attends the Cathedral Latin School.

Ca. 1591

Begins to study under the Antwerp painters Tobias Verhaecht (a landscape artist), then Adam van Noort and, finally, with Otto van Veen.

1598

Becomes a Master of the Antwerp Guild of St. Luke.

1600

9 May: Leaves for Italy. For the next eight years he serves as Court Painter to the Duke of Mantua, Vincenzo Gonzaga.

1603

3 (or 5) March: Leaves Mantua and sets out for Spain. With him he takes works of art intended as presents for the Spanish King Philip II and the Duke of Lerma, the latter's premier minister. Paints *The Duke of Lerma on Horseback* (Prado, Madrid).

1604

June: Returns to Italy.

38. ***The Death of Henri IV and the Proclamation of the Regency***. 1622, oil on wood, 48 x 65 cm, The Hermitage, St. Petersburg.

39. *Self-Portrait with his wife Isabelle Brandt.* Alte Pinakothek, Munich.

40. *Portrait of a Lady-in-Waiting to the Infanta Isabella.* 1623-1625, oil on wood, 64 x 48 cm, The Hermitage, St. Petersburg.

1606-1608

Lives and works in Rome where he is commissioned to paint an altarpiece for the Church of S. Maria in Vallicella (Chiesa Nuova) by the Oratorian Congregation: *The Madonna Adored by Saints* (original version is in the Musée de Peinture et Sculpture, Grenoble; the finished work is in said church).

1608

28 October: Leaves Rome after learning of the fatal illness of his mother. Arrives in Antwerp about 11 December.

1609

23 September: Appointed Court Painter to the Habsburg Regents in Flanders, Archduke Albert and the Infanta Isabella.
3 October: Marries Isabella, the daughter of Jan Brant, an Antwerp barrister.

1609-1610

Paints *Self-portrait with Isabella Brant* (Alte Pinakothek, Munich)(p.56); on commission from the Antwerp city council executes the painting *The Adoration of the Magi* (Prado, Madrid)(p.79) for the Council Chamber of the Town Hall.

1610

Buys a house in Antwerp and over the next few years rebuilds and decorates it according to his own design (now the Rubenshuis, Antwerp).

1610-1611

Produces the triptych *The Elevation of the Cross* (Antwerp Cathedral) for the Church of St Walpurgis. Has a great many apprentices in his workshop.

1611-1614

Produces the triptych *The Descent from the Cross* (p.32) for the altar of Arquebusiers in Antwerp Cathedral (now Antwerp Cathedral).

1617

Works on a painting for a series of tapestries, *The History of the Consul Decius Mus* (Liechtensteinische Staatliche Kunstsammlung, Vaduz).

41. ***The Apotheosis of James I***. Around 1630, oil on canvas, 89.7 x 55.3 cm, The Hermitage, St. Petersburg.

1620

29 March: Signs a contract to sketch 39 compositions for ceilings in the Jesuit Church in Antwerp (burnt down in 1718).

1622

February: Concludes an agreement with Marie de' Medici, the widow of Henry IV, to produce a large series of paintings for the gallery of the Luxembourg Palace in Paris: *The Life of Marie de' Medici* (Louvre, Paris). Publishes I *Palazzi di Genova* in Antwerp, a collection of engravings of "plans, façades and cross-sections" based on his drawings.

42. **Helene Fourment.**
1630-1631,
oil on canvas,
163.5 x 137 cm, Alte
Pinakothek, Munich.

43. **The Vision of St. Ildefonso.** Triptych.
Kunsthistorisches
Museum, Vienna.

44. *The Vision of St. Ildefonso.* 1630-1631, oil on canvas, 52 x 83 cm, The Hermitage, St. Petersburg.

1622-1623

Draws 12 cartoons for the series of tapestries *The History of Constantine* commissioned by Louis XIII (cartoons not extant).

1623

The Infanta Isabella, Vice-Regent of Flanders, decrees that Rubens shall receive a monthly allowance. Begins his activities as a diplomat.

1624

29 January: Raised to the nobility.

1626

20 June: Death of Isabella Brant.

1627

Travels to Holland to meet Balthazar Gerbier, an English diplomat agent.

1627-1628

On the Infanta Isabella's commission completes 15 cartoons for the series of tapestries *The Triumph of the Eucharist* (3 cartoons are in the Ringling Museum, Sarasota, Fla.).

1628

28 (or 29) August: Travels from Antwerp on a diplomatic mission. There paints *Portrait of Philip V on Horseback* (non extant).

1629

27 April: Appointed Secretary of the Spanish King's Privy Council for Flanders. 13 May: Returns from Spain to Brussels. 5 June: Arrives in London to conduct peace negotiations between Spain and England.

45. ***The Last Supper***.
1631-1632, oil on wood, 48.8 x 41 cm, The Pushkin Museum of Fine Arts, Moscow.

1629-1630

Paints the allegorical *Peace and War* (National Gallery, London) which he presents to Charles I. He is commissioned by Charles to produce 9 ceiling paintings for the Banqueting House in Whitehall, London (still extant).

46. *Landscape with a Rainbow*. 1632-1635, oil on canvas, 86 x 130 cm, The Hermitage, St. Petersburg.

1630

3 March: Knighted by Charles I. Made an honorary Master of Arts by Cambridge University.

6 April: Returns from London to Antwerp.

6 December: Marries Helene Fourment, the younger daughter of a rich dealer in tapestries, Daniel Fourment.

1631

20 August: Knighted by Philip IV of Spain.

1634-1635

Commissioned by the city council of Antwerp, he works on sketches of triumphal arches for the ceremonial reception of the new Governor, the Cardinal Infante Ferdinand, on 17 April 1635 (Hermitage, St Petersburg; Pushkin Museum, Moscow; Fogg Museum, Cambridge; Ashmolen Museum, Oxford; Koninklijk Museum voor schone Konsten, Antwerp; Musée de Bonnat, Bayonne).

1635

Buys the Château de Steen near Elewijt where he mainly spends the summer months. His final landscapes are painted in the locality.

1636

June: Made Court Painter to the Cardinal Infante Ferdinand. Receives a commission for 112 paintings on themes from Ovid's *Metamorphoses* for Philip IV's hunting lodge Torre de la Parada, near Madrid (most of the paintings are in the Prado, Madrid).

1637-1638

Paints *The Horrors of War* (Pitti, Florence).

1640

27 May: Writes his will.

30 May: Peter Paul Rubens dies.

47. ***Felicitations on the Arrival of the Infante Ferdinand in Antwerp***. 1634-1635, oil on wood, 73 x 78 cm, The Hermitage, St. Petersburg.

48. ***The Arch of Ferdinand***. 1634, oil on wood, 104 x 72.5 cm, The Hermitage, St. Petersburg.

49. ***The Temple of Janus***. 1634, oil on wood, 70 x 65.5 cm, The Hermitage, St. Petersburg.

50. *Mercury Leaving
    Antwerp*. 1634,
    oil on wood,
    76 x 79 cm,
    The Hermitage,
    St. Petersburg.

51. *The Arch of
    Hercules*. 1634-1635,
    oil on canvas,
    150 x 73 cm,
    The Hermitage,
    St. Petersburg.

52. **Bacchus**.
   Oil on canvas,
   191 x 161.3 cm,
   The Hermitage,
   St. Petersburg.

53. **Pastoral Scene**.
   1636-1640,
   oil on canvas,
   114 x 91 cm,
   The Hermitage,
   St. Petersburg.

54. *Landscape with Simon and Iphigenie*. Late 1630s, oil on wood, 49 x 73 cm, The Hermitage, St. Petersburg.

NOTES

1.   G. Mancini, *Cansiderazioni sulla pittura*, vols. I-II, Rome, 1956-1957; see the Latin odes of the Leyden Professors, Daniel Heinsius and Dominicus Baudius (1609 and 1612), and the Dutch verse of Anna Rumors Fischer (1621) in CDR 1887-1909, II, pp. 12, 55-57, 330, 331.

2.   Bottari (1768) considered that the letter was written around 1630; Haskell (1963), citing B. Nicholson, suggests an approximate dating to 1620. (See G. Bottari, *Raccolta di lettera sulla pittura, scultura ed architettura*, vol. VI, Rome, 1768, p. 751; and F. Haskell, Patrons and Painters, London, 1963, p. 94).

3.   G. P. Bellori, *Le Vite de pittori, scultori ed architetti moderni*, Rome, 1728, p. 150.

4.   Roger de Piles 1677, pp. 77-107, 227-290.

5.   J.-J. Winckelmann, *Gedanken über die Nachahmungen der griechischen Werke...* Dresden and Leipzig, 1756, pp. 123-124.

6.   W. Heinse, "Über einige Gemälde der Düsseldorfer Galerie. An Herrn Canonicus Gleim", *Der Teutsche Merkur*, 1777, No. 5, May, pp. 131-135; No. 7, July, pp. 60-90.

7.   W. Goethe, "'Nach Falconet und über Falconet'. Aus Goethes Brieftasche (1775)", *Sämtliche Werke*. Jubiläumsausgabe, vol. XXXIII, p. 40.

8.   Fr. Schlegel, "Gemäldebeschreibungen aus Paris und den Niederlanden", 1802-1804, *Sämtliche Werke*, vol. VI, Vienna, 1823, p. 192.

9.   E. Delacroix, *Journal*. Paris, 1865.

10.   E. Fromentin, *Les Maîtres d'autrefois*, Paris, 1965.

11.   A. van Hasselt, *Histoire de P. P. Rubens...*, Brussels, 1840, pp. 2, 26-27, 39, 40, 180.

12.   F. Jos van den Branden, *Geschiedenes der Antwerpsche Schilderschool...*, Antwerp, 1883, pp. V-VI, 497, 499, 501.

13.   *CDR* 1887-1909, vols. I-VI.

14.   Rooses 1886-1892, vols. I-V; see also the *Corpus Diplomaticus Rubenianum Ludwig Burchard* (Brussels), which is being published. To date the following volumes of the Corpus have been issued: I, 1968; II, 1978; VII, 1984; VIII, 1972; IX, 1971; X, 1975; XV, 1987; XVI, 1972; XVIII, I, 1982; XIX, 1977; XXI, 1977; XXIII, 1986; XXIV, 1980. When complete the Corpus will consist of 26 volumes and provide an exhaustive record of Rubens' works and of documents associated with his art.

15.   Smith 1830-1842, vols. II, IX.

16.   V.-S. 1873.

17.   J. Burckhardt, *Erinnerungen an Rubens*, Basle, 1898, passim.

18.   R. Oldenbourg, "Die Nachwirkung Italiens auf Rubens und die Gründung seiner Werkstatt", in R. Oldenbourg, *Peter Paul Rubens*, Munich and Berlin, 1922, p. 12.

19.   G. Hanotaux, "Richelieu et Rubens", in G. Hanotaux, *Sur les chemins de l'histoire*, vol. 1, Paris, 1924, p. 272.

20.   L. van Puyvelde, *Le Génie de Rubens*, Brussels, 1943, pp. 20, 27.

21.   Quoted from: J. Burckhardt, *Erinnerungen an Rubens*. Leipzig, 1928, p. 130.

55. **The Adoration of the Three Kings**.
Prado, Madrid

LIST OF ILLUSTRATIONS